ELECTRONICS POCKET BOOK

by Bill Bay

© 1981 by Mel Bay Publications, Inc.
Pacific, MO. 63069. International Copyright Secured.
All Rights Reserved. Printed in U.S.A.

CONTENTS

Tuning the Bass	3 & 4
The Left Hand	5
The Right Hand	6
Guide to Chord Diagrams	7
Chord Symbol Abbreviations	8
C Chords	9
C#/Db Chords	10
D Chords	11
Da/Eb Chords	12
E Chords	13
F Chords	14
Fa/Gb Chords	15
G Chords	16
Ga/Ab Chords	17
A Chords	18
Aa/Bb Chords	19
B Chords	20
Types of Notes	21
Rests	22
Time Signatures	23
Fingerboard Diagram	24 & 25
How to Read Tablature	26
Walkin' Blues	27
Drivin' Bass	28
Bass Riff	29
Fusion Line	30
All Purpose Bass Riffs	32

TUNING THE ELECTRIC BASS

3

The four open strings of the Bass will be the same pitch as the four notes shown in the illustration of the piano keyboard. Note that all of the strings are below middle C of the piano keyboard.

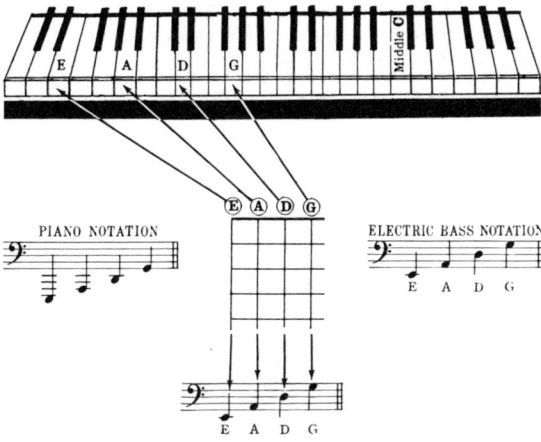

ANOTHER METHOD OF TUNING

1. Tune the 4th string in unison to the E or 19th white key to the left of middle C on the piano.

2. Place the finger behind the fifth fret of the 4th string. This will give you the tone or pitch of the 3rd string (A).

3. Place finger behind the fifth fret of the 3rd string to obtain the pitch of the 2nd string (D).

4. Place the finger behind the fifth fret of the 2nd string to obtain the pitch of the first string (G).

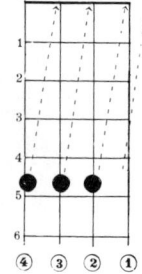

O = Open String

① = String Number

THE LEFT HAND   5

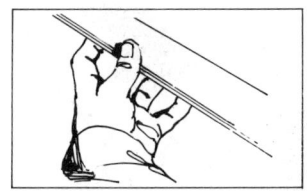 

Place the thumb on the center part of the neck. This allows the fingers to press the strings directly on the finger tips and it allows for easier left hand movement up and down the neck.

THE RIGHT HAND

Fig. 1

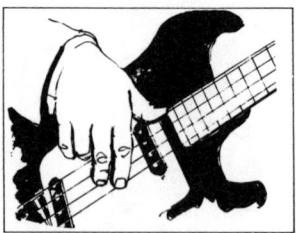

Fig. 2

Alternate the 1st and 2nd fingers. Pull the fingers straight across the strings. Some bassists rest the thumb on the body or aginst the 4th string (Fig. 2)

Guide To Chord Diagrams

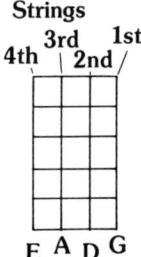

Strings
4th 3rd 2nd 1st
E A D G

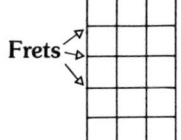

Frets

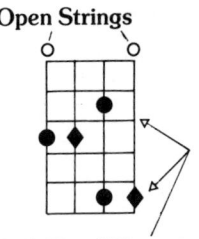

Open Strings

Left Hand Fingering

♦ = Root of Chord

CHORD SYMBOL ABBREVIATIONS

Major = C, F, G, etc.
Minor = Cm, Fm, etc.
Diminished = C°, Cdim, C−, etc.
Augmented = C+, C aug. etc.

Dominant Seventh = C_7, F_7, etc.
Sixth = C_6, F_6, etc.
Minor 7th = Cm_7, Fm_7, etc.
Minor 6th = Cm_6, Fm_6, etc.

Major 7th = Cma_7, $C\bar{7}$
Dominant Seventh Sharp Fifth = $C_7 + 5$, $C_7 \#5$, etc.
Dominant Seventh Flat Fifth = $C_7 - 5$, $C_7 b5$, etc.
Minor Seventh F,T Fifth = $Cm_7 - 5$, $Cm_7 b5$, etc.
Seventh Suspended Fourth = $C_7 sus4$, $C_7 sus$, etc.

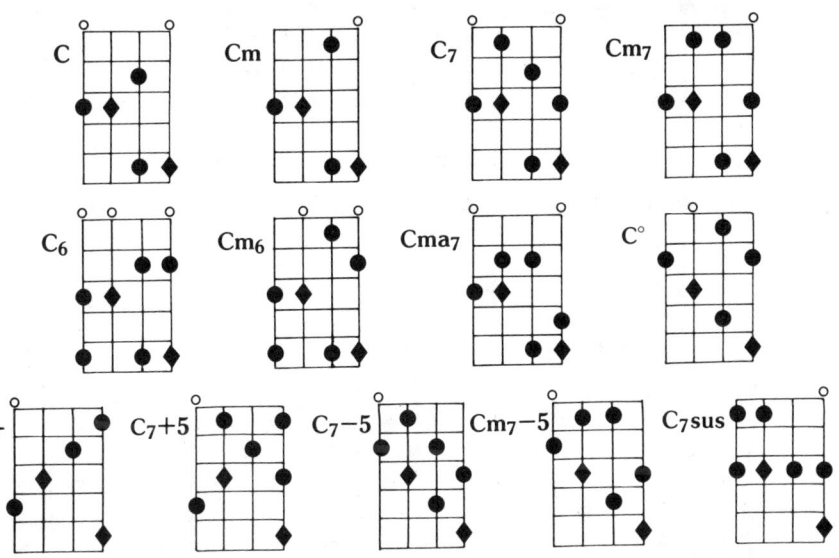

C#/D♭

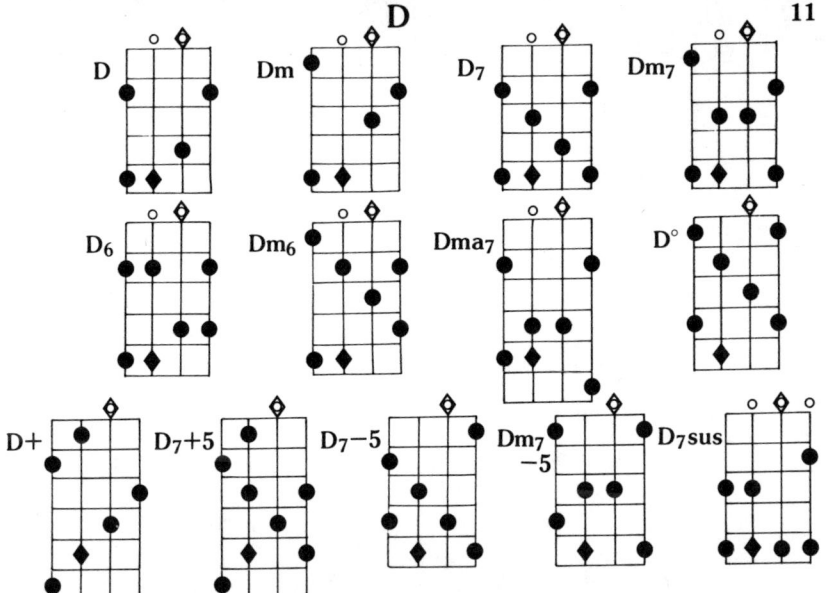

D♯/E♭

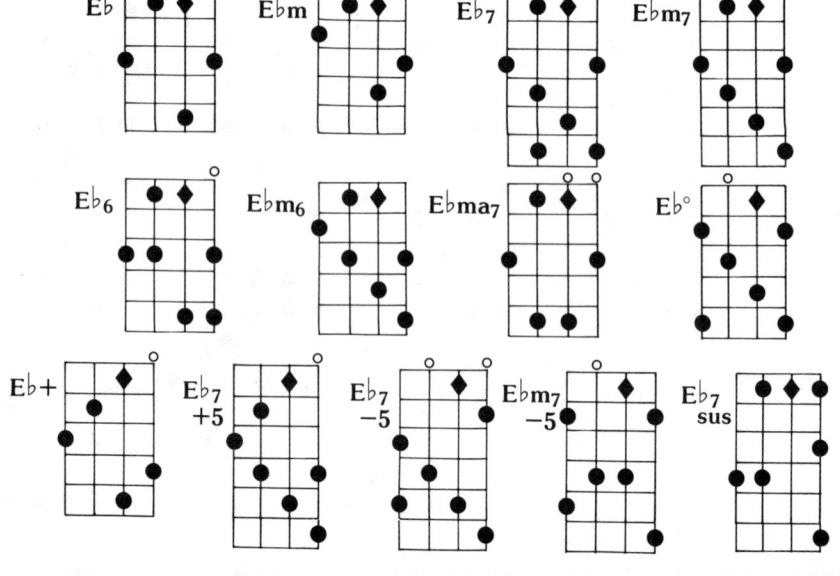

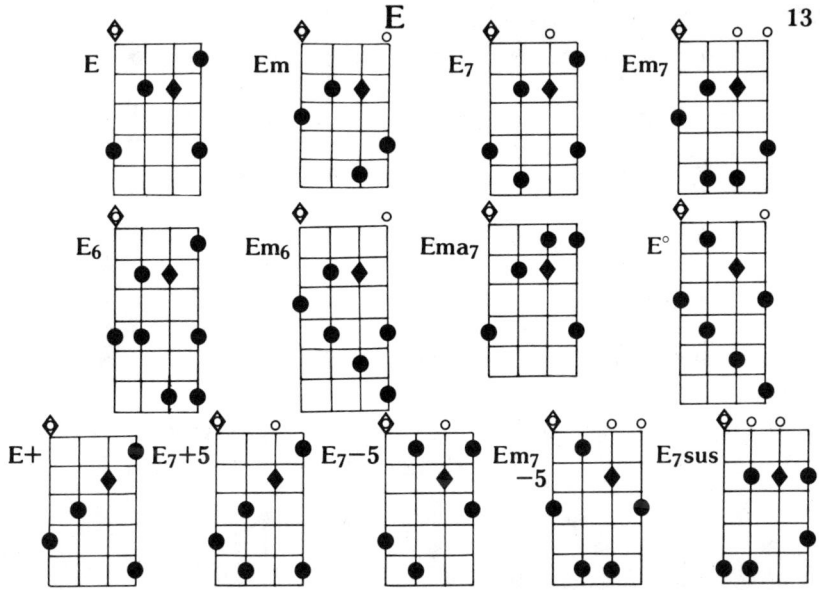

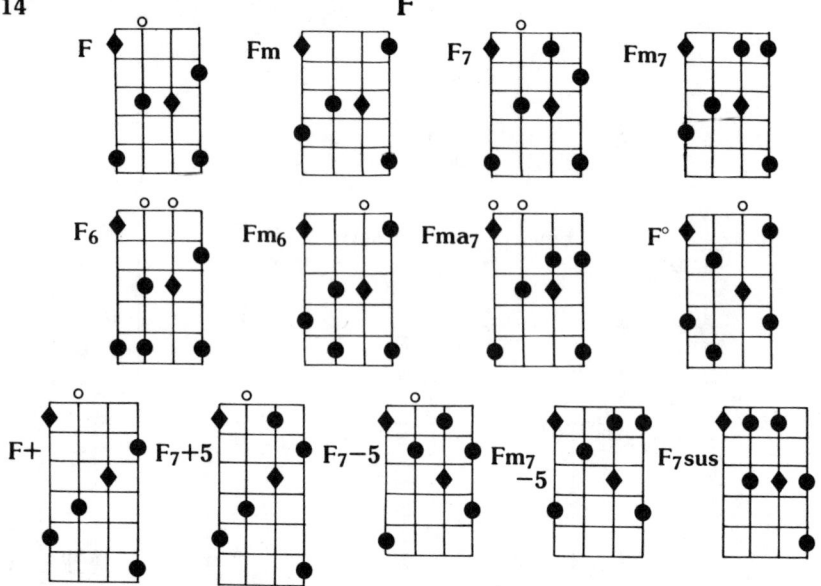

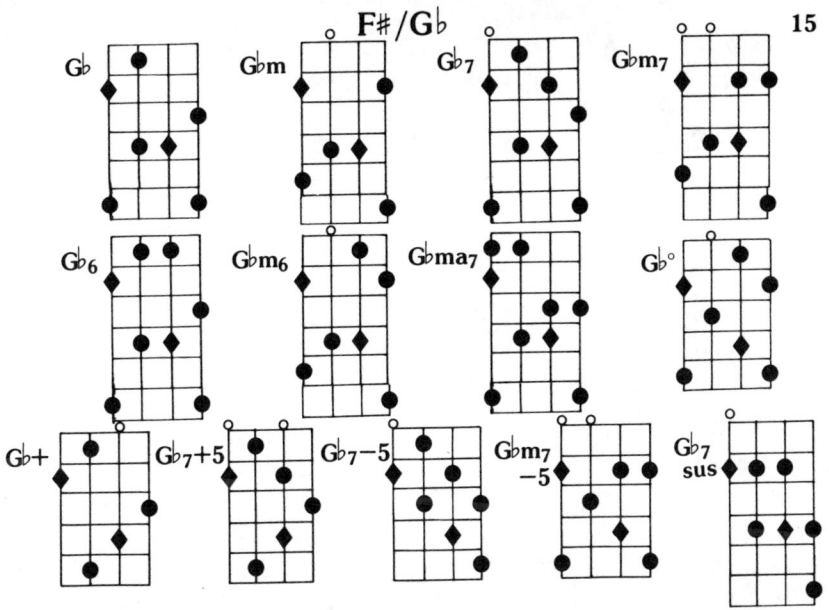

G

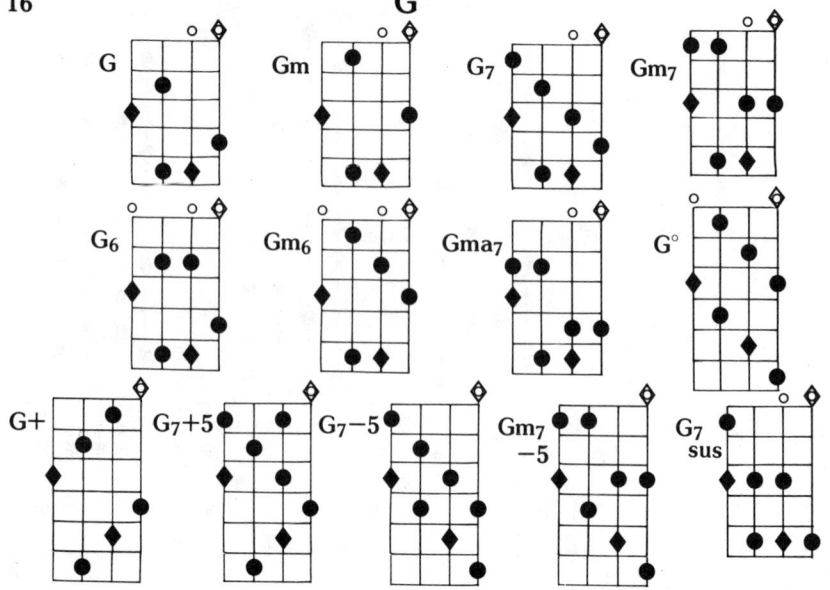

G#/A♭

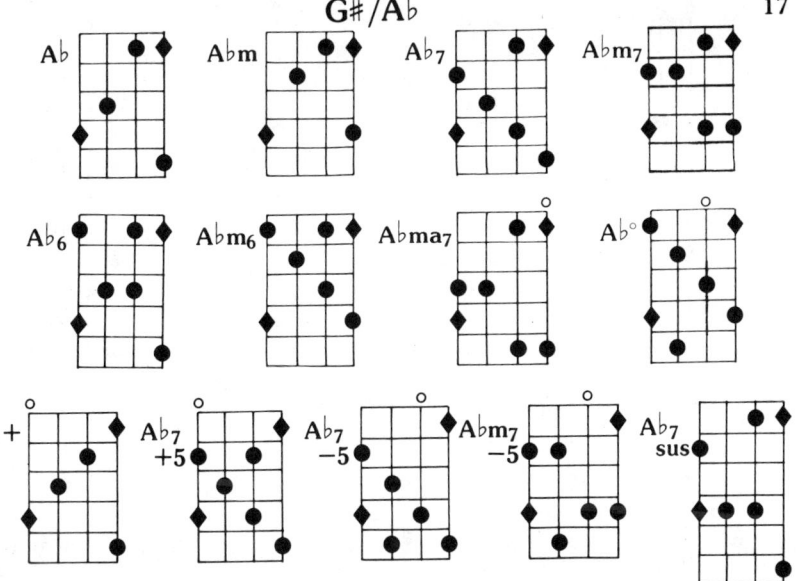

A

A
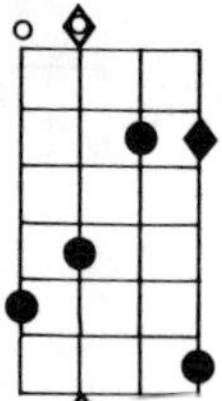

Am
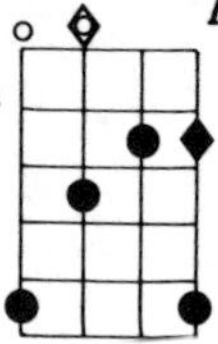

A7
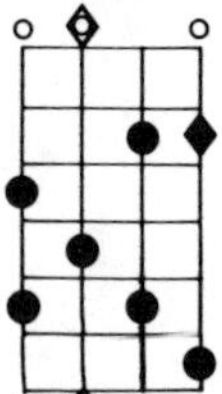

Am7
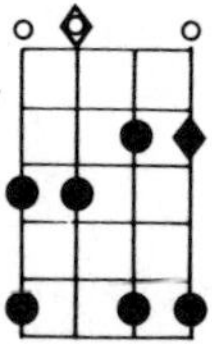

A6
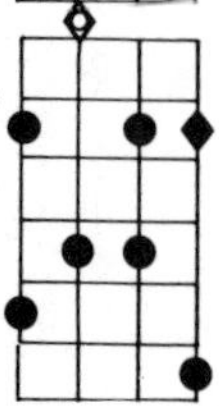

Am6
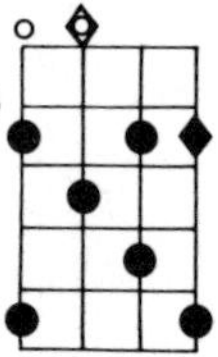

Ama7
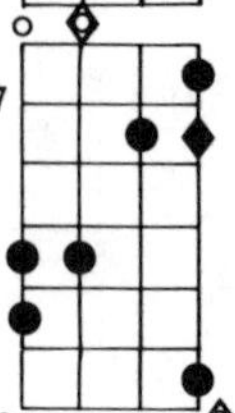

A°
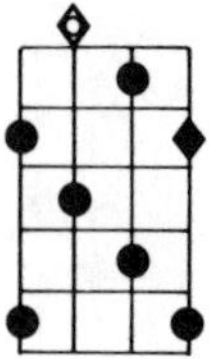

A+
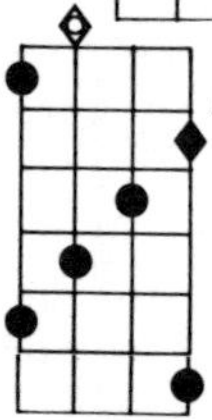

A7+5
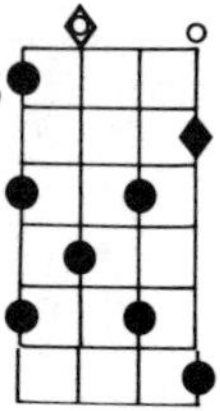

A7−5
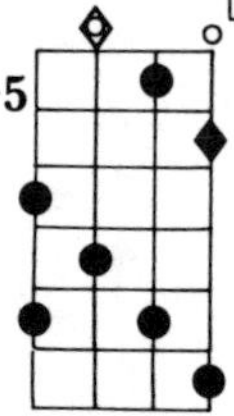

Am7 −5
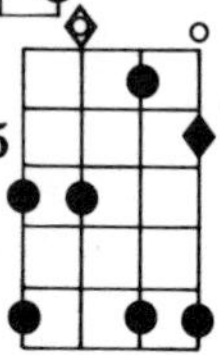

A7sus
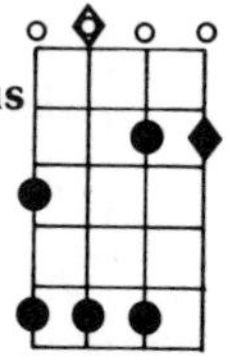

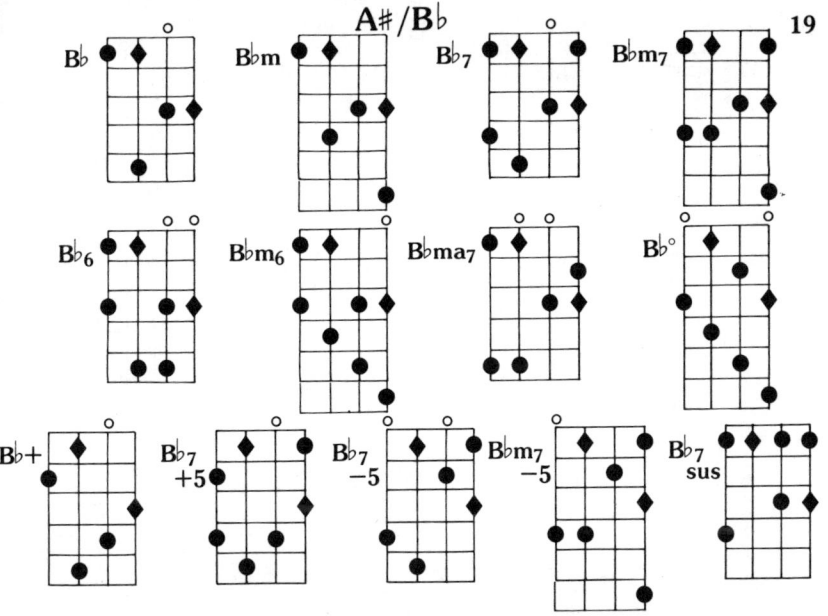

20 B

B	Bm	B₇	Bm₇
Bm₆	Bma₇	B°
B+	B₇+5	B₇−5	Bm₇−5	B₇sus

TYPES OF NOTES

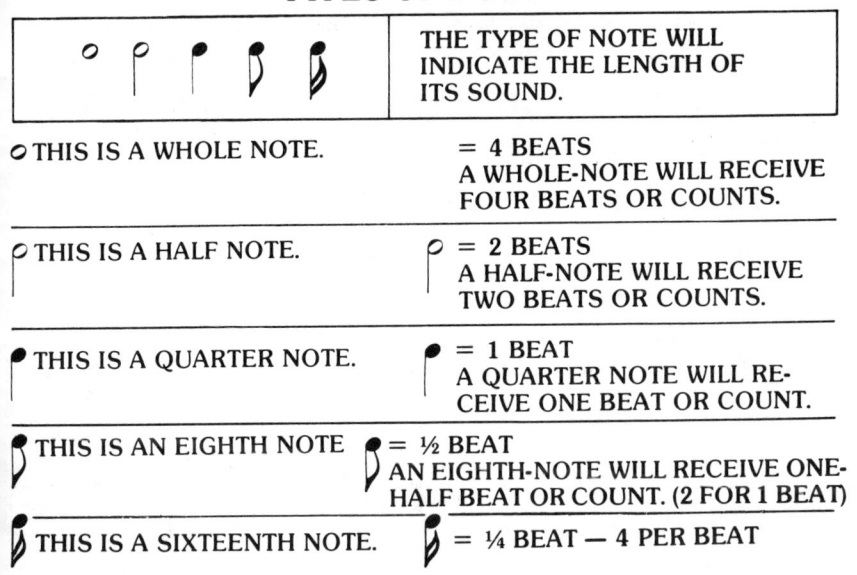

o ♩ ♩ ♪ ♪	THE TYPE OF NOTE WILL INDICATE THE LENGTH OF ITS SOUND.

○ THIS IS A WHOLE NOTE.   = 4 BEATS
A WHOLE-NOTE WILL RECEIVE FOUR BEATS OR COUNTS.

♩ THIS IS A HALF NOTE.   ♩ = 2 BEATS
A HALF-NOTE WILL RECEIVE TWO BEATS OR COUNTS.

♩ THIS IS A QUARTER NOTE.   ♩ = 1 BEAT
A QUARTER NOTE WILL RECEIVE ONE BEAT OR COUNT.

♪ THIS IS AN EIGHTH NOTE   ♪ = ½ BEAT
AN EIGHTH-NOTE WILL RECEIVE ONE-HALF BEAT OR COUNT. (2 FOR 1 BEAT)

♪ THIS IS A SIXTEENTH NOTE.   ♪ = ¼ BEAT — 4 PER BEAT

RESTS

A REST is a sign to designate a period of silence. This period of silence will be of the same duration as the note to which it corresponds.

𝄾 **THIS IS AN EIGHTH REST**

𝄿 **THIS IS A SIXTEENTH REST**

𝄽 **THIS IS A QUARTER REST**

▬ **THIS IS A HALF REST**
Note that it lays on the line.

▬ **THIS IS A WHOLE REST**
Note that it hangs down from the line.

NOTES

WHOLE	HALF	QUARTER	EIGHTH	SIXTEENTH
4 COUNTS	2 COUNTS	1 COUNT	2 FOR 1 COUNT	4 FOR 1 COUNT

RESTS

THE TIME SIGNATURE

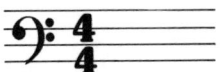  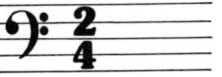

The above examples are the common types of time signatures to be used in this book.

4   The top number indicates the number of beats per measure   **4**   beats per measure

4   The bottom number indicates the type of note receiving one beat beats per measure   **4**   a quarter-note receives one beat.

6   BEATS PER MEASURE
8   EACH EIGHTH-NOTE RECEIVES ONE FULL BEAT

Signifies so called "common time" and is simply another way of designating $\frac{4}{4}$ time.

BASIC NOTES

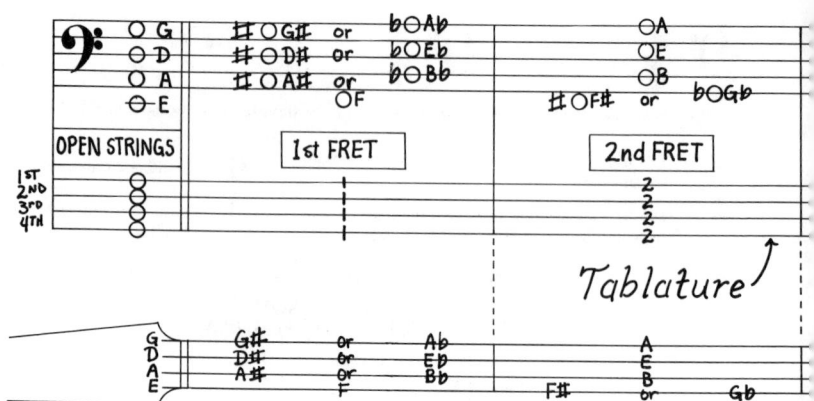

ON THE BASS

3rd FRET	4th FRET	5th FRET

String notes at 3rd fret (top staff, high to low): #○A# or b○Bb / ○F / ○C / ○G
String notes at 4th fret: ○B / #○F# or ○Gb / #○C# or b○Db / #○G# or b○Ab
String notes at 5th fret: ○C / ○G / ○D / ○A

(LINES = STRINGS)
(NUMBERS = FRETS)

Bottom staff notes:
- 3rd fret: A# or Bb / F / C / G
- 4th fret: B / F# or Gb / C# or Db / G# or Ab
- 5th fret: C / G / D / A

HOW TO READ TABLATURE

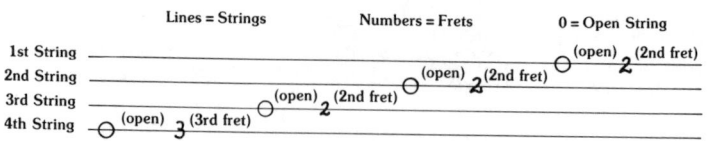

RHYTHM IN TABLATURE

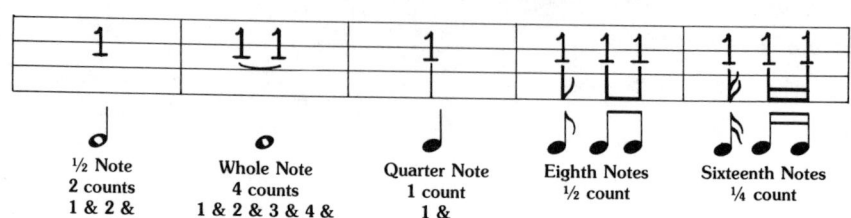

BASS RIFF

FUSION LINE

31